Take up
NEEDLEPOINT

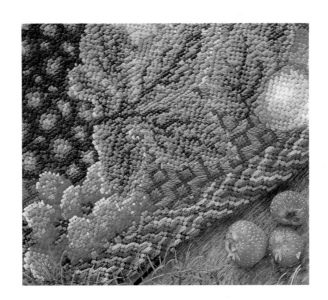

Take up NEEDLEPOINT

JILL GORDON

KÖNEMANN

Published in 1994 by
Merehurst Limited
Ferry House, 51 – 57 Lacy Road
Putney, London SW 15 1PR

Edited by Alison Wormleighton
Designed by Kit Johnson
Photography by Di Lewis
Illustrations by Paul Bryant
Charts by King & King

Typesetting by
Litho Link Limited, Welshpool, Powys
Colour seperation by
Fotographics Ltd,
UK – Hong Kong

Copyright © 1999 for this edition
Könemann Verlagsgesellschaft mbH
Bonner Str. 126, D- 50968 Cologne

Production Manager: Detlev Schaper
Assistants: Nicola Leurs, Alexandra Kiesling
Printing and Binding:
Sing Cheong Printing Co Ltd., Hong Kong
Printed in Hong Kong China

ISBN 3-8290-2786-9
10 9 8 7 6 5 4 3 2 1

CONTENTS

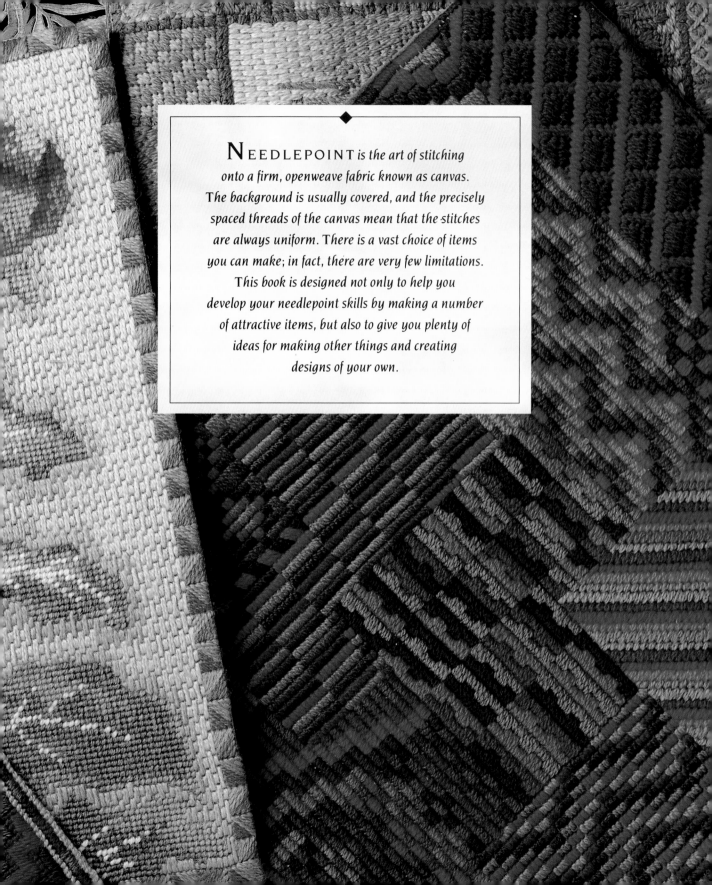

NEEDLEPOINT is the art of stitching
onto a firm, openweave fabric known as canvas.
The background is usually covered, and the precisely
spaced threads of the canvas mean that the stitches
are always uniform. There is a vast choice of items
you can make; in fact, there are very few limitations.
This book is designed not only to help you
develop your needlepoint skills by making a number
of attractive items, but also to give you plenty of
ideas for making other things and creating
designs of your own.

Materials and Equipment

To do justice to your needlepoint and obtain a
professional finish, it is important to use high-quality materials,
but you do not need very much expensive or
space-consuming equipment.

Canvas

When buying canvas you should consider the colour you wish to work on. Stitching on white canvas with small holes can be very tiring to the eyes, but white is still the best colour to choose if you are working with very pale yarns, as a dark canvas could show through. The type of stitch you are using is another factor to take into consideration when choosing the colour of your canvas. Random straight stitch, for example, often leaves some canvas showing, so it is usually better to use a fawn-coloured canvas (known as 'antique').

Needlepoint canvas is made from cotton, linen or synthetic fibres. It comes in many different shapes and sizes but there are three main types:

Single-thread plain canvas is constructed from evenly spaced single threads woven over and under each other. Sometimes the term 'mono' is used rather than 'single thread', and 'regular' or 'interwoven' instead of plain. Because the threads are not bound together, this type of canvas has good give, making it suitable for cushions but not for chair seats or similar items which would soon stretch too much. One of the drawbacks to this canvas is that the threads or meshes are not interlocked, which means that if, for instance, tent stitch is used you must be sure that it always *is* tent stitch and goes over two threads at the back so that it cannot unravel; half cross stitch, which only goes over one thread at the back, cannot be used.

Interlock canvas is also constructed from single threads but they actually pass through each other at the points where they intersect. This type of canvas does not have the give that evenweave does and so is fairly suitable for cushions and well-upholstered seats. It is particularly useful because it does not unravel, making it ideal for small items that need to be trimmed close to the stitched area.

Double-thread canvas, also known as Penelope canvas, has a double-mesh construction – ie, pairs of horizontal threads intersect pairs of vertical threads. This makes it strong and hardwearing, and therefore ideal for chair seats and other items where some strain will be put on the canvas. It also means that it can be used for finely detailed work because the pairs of threads can be separated, and for work combining finely detailed stitches (known as petitpoint) with a large stitch (grospoint). The grospoint areas are worked over pairs of threads, and the petitpoint areas over single threads which have been separated. In 19th century needlepoints, figures or flowers were often worked in petitpoint, while the background was in grospoint.

Note: In this book, when the instructions refer to a 'thread' of double-thread canvas, it means a pair of threads. Also, the canvas suggested for each project is the type actually used in the photograph, but a different type could be substituted if preferred.

The closer together the threads of canvas are, the smaller the needlepoint stitches will be. The number of threads per 2.5cm (1in) is known as the gauge of the canvas. Thus, the higher the gauge, the smaller the stitch. A 14-gauge canvas, for example, which is very popular for general work, has 14 threads to 2.5cm (1in). Although canvasses can be bought in many different gauges, they are grouped into two ranges: petitpoint canvasses, which have 16 or more threads to 2.5cm (1in), and grospoint canvasses, which have fewer than that.

To get the most pleasure from your needlepoint projects, it is important to choose a gauge of canvas that you enjoy working with. All but one of the projects in this book are worked on fairly large-holed canvas so that the work progresses relatively quickly and you can learn new stitches more easily. (The trinket box lid on pages 16–17, which is worked on 16-gauge canvas, is the only project that uses small-holed canvas.)

Yarns

Needlepoint can be worked in any type of thread, as long as it can be threaded easily and passes through the canvas without difficulty. The most commonly used thread is wool, which is sold as tapestry wool, crewel wool or Persian yarn.

Tapestry wool can be used just as it comes, to cover average (10–14) gauge canvas. It cannot be split into separate plys. Tapestry wool comes in 25g (1oz) hanks and small skeins.

Crewel wool is used as single strands to cover fine gauges or double strands for slightly larger ones. It comes in 25g (1oz) hanks and in small skeins.

Persian yarn is extremely versatile, as it can be used as it comes (three threads twisted together to form a single strand) or can be split and used as single or double strands, depending on the gauge of canvas. It is also interesting to mix three shades together for subtle effects. It generally comes in small skeins and 100g (4oz) hanks.

The chart shown below gives a rough idea of how many threads are needed for different gauges of canvas. It is only an approximate guide because the yarn that will cover the canvas will depend upon the stitch you are using.

The projects in this book use only wool, but nice effects can also be achieved with embroidery silks, metallic threads and ribbons.

Tools and equipment

Tapestry needles should be used rather than ordinary large needles, as tapestry needles have a blunt point to avoid splitting canvas threads. Needles come in sizes 13 (the largest) to 24 (the finest); size 18 is the most commonly used. The size you should use depends on the canvas – the needle needs to pass easily through the holes in the canvas without distorting them. The appropriate size for the most popuar canvasses is shown in the chart below

Whether or not you use a frame is a matter of personal preference. Hand-held and floor-standing frames are both available. The advantages of a frame are that the work does not distort as much while you are working on it, and some complicated stitches are easier to work while the canvas is taut. The disadvantages are loss of speed and the fact that you cannot carry your work around with you as easily. Hoops are only suitable for fine-gauge, soft canvasses.

Large scissors for cutting canvas are useful, and you'll also need some small, sharp scissors for the work itself.

Make sure that you work in good light. If you are able to work only at times when artificial light is needed, an anglepoise lamp wih a daylight simulation bulb in it makes working a lot more pleasant. Lamps with built-in magnification are also available. At any rate, ordinary overhead lighting is not sufficient for needlepoint.

SUITABILITY OF CANVASSES, YARNS AND NEEDLES

CANVAS	YARN (no. of strands and type)	NEEDLE SIZE
Single (mono) 22 or 24	I crewel I Persian	24
Single (mono) 18	I crewel I Persian	22 or 24
Single (mono) 16	2 crewel I or 2 Persian	22
Single (mono) 14 or 12	3 crewel 2 Persian I tapestry yarn	20
Double (Penelope) 10	3 or 4 crewel 2 or 3 Persian I tapestry yarn I tapestry yarn with I crewel	20 or 18
Single (mono) or double (Penelope) 8, 7, or 6	I tapestry yarn with I crewel 3 or 4 Persian	18 or 16

Basic Techniques

*The best way to learn needlepoint is by actually
doing it, but before you embark on your first stitches,
there are a few general tips and techniques
you need to know about.*

Preparation

When measuring the canvas, leave 5cm (2in) extra on each side for stretching it when the work is finished. Always cut it following the same thread along the canvas, otherwise it will unravel, wasting canvas. Once you have cut the canvas, it is a good idea to put masking tape on the raw edges or to hem them or sew on bias binding so that you don't keep catching your yarn on the rough edges while you are working.

It is useful to mark with an arrow which way up the design is so that you always know in which direction you are working. Otherwise, if you have to keep putting your work down to do other things (as is inevitable) it is all too easy to pick it up and start stitching in the wrong direction.

Use lengths of yarn that are no longer than 50cm (20in); anything longer becomes worn, weak and thin, giving insufficient coverage.

There is no need to use knots; they create a very uneven texture and make it more difficult to stretch the finished work. To begin without a knot, bring the needle up through the hole in the canvas where you wish to make the first stitch, while holding a 2.5cm (1in) tail of wool underneath with your other hand. Form the first stitch and pull it firm, holding the tail so that the stitch cannot pull through, then form the second and subsequent stitches so as to catch in the tail on the underside.

Similarly, when finishing a strand of thread, darn it in neatly on the underside of the canvas and cut off any remaining end.

When moving with one colour from one area of canvas to another, provided it is not too far away, thread the yarn through the underside of the stitching so that you do not have any untidy loops left hanging. If you wish to use the same colour at some distance away, it is better to finish the thread off and then begin it again in the new place.

Stitching

Working the stitches using the sewing method – in which the movements of pulling the needle and thread through to the back side and then pulling them through to the right side are done in one scooping movement – is the easiest and quickest way to learn needlepoint, particularly tent stitch. The so-called stabbing method, which involves two movements for each stitch, is effective when using a frame or when working the more intricate stitches. In this book the diagrams used to illustrate the stitches show the sewing method.

Be aware of stitch tension as you work. Tension that is too tight will distort the canvas threads and therefore the design and also make the yarn too thin so that it doesn't cover the canvas adequately. Tension that is too loose, however, will make the stitches stand away from the surface.

Using charts

Most of the instructions for the projects in this book, and many other needlepoint patterns you will come across, are in chart form.

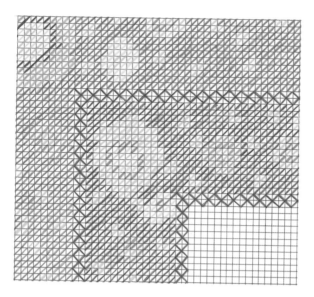

◆ *The main type of needlepoint chart: a box chart*

A **box chart** is the most frequently used chart for a wide variety of stitches. On it, each *square* represents one *stitch*. The squares either are coloured in or contain a symbol to indicate the colour and type of yarn, and sometimes the stitch if more than one stitch is used. A square on a box chart represents one canvas intersection – ie, a vertical thread and a horizontal thread intersecting – *not* a hole in the canvas.

A **line chart** is more often used for ornamental stitches. On it, the grid lines correspond to the canvas threads, and the yarns/stitches are indicated by thick lines actually drawn over the intersections as the stitches should be worked. The lines either are in colour or incorporate symbols.

There are no standard symbols, but one or more keys will appear with the charts. A key to the stitches used in the charts in this book appears on page 71.

Where only part of a chart is given, it means that the rest of the design consists of repeats of that portion, either identical or a mirror image of it. Many geometrical designs are symmetrical and so only a quarter or a half of the chart needs to be shown.

If a chart is the same size as the needlepoint will be, you can place it under the canvas and draw the outline on the canvas with a permanent marker. If not, either enlarge it on a photocopier or count threads on the pattern and canvas. You may wish to mark the canvas and chart into groups of ten threads by ten threads.

Blocking and setting

Because your needlepoint will inevitably become distorted as you work, especially if you are not using a frame, it's necessary on completion to block, or stretch, it and then set it. The process involves smoothing and stretching it back into shape, then damping the canvas so it redries in the correct shape.

First make a template out of brown paper or thin cardboard to the dimensions your work is intended to be. Obtain a piece of wood at least 10cm (4in) bigger all the way around than the finished work plus bare canvas border, so that you will have room to pull the work into shape and to nail it in position. Place a piece of undyed cotton or similar fabric on top of the wood, then lay your work on it, face down. Dampen the back of the work evenly using a plant mister or sponge. (Be sparing with water when dampening silks. Tapestry yarn is normally colourfast, but it is as well not to dampen them too liberally.)

Using your template to guide you, pull the work into shape. Using 5cm (2in) rustproof nails, hammer in a nail at the centre of each side about 4cm (1½in) from the stitching, then work out to the corners, keeping the edges of the work straight, and making sure the corners form right angles if they are supposed to, Put in enough nails for them to be no more than about 2cm (¾in) apart.

Once it is stretched into the required shape, paint the back of the canvas with ordinary wallpaper paste, using a large brush. Leave the canvas on the board in a warm place until completely dry (at least 48 hours), then pull the nails out with the claw of the hammer.

Protecting your work

Fabric protectors such as Scotchgard can be useful for protecting your handiwork if it will be vulnerable to stains, as in a placemat, for example. However, be sure always to test the product on some of the yarn, as some can make colours run.

MARKING THE CENTRE POINT

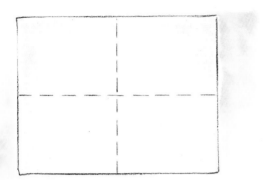

♦ Needlepoint designs should be worked from the centre outwards. Find the centre of one edge of the canvas and work a line of running stitches, as shown, from the centre to the opposite side. (Or, if you prefer, mark the line with a permanent marker pen.) Do the same for the other dimension. The two lines cross at the centre of the canvas.

THREADING A NEEDLE

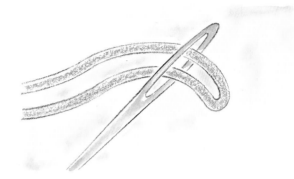

♦ To thread a tapestry needle with yarn, loop one end of the yarn over the eye end of the needle, holding it tightly between your thumb and first finger to form a fold, then remove the needle. Now push this fold through the eye of the needle. Needle-threading tools are available if you find this fiddly.

MITRING CORNERS

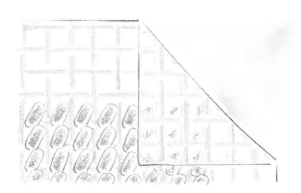

1 ♦ To mitre the corners of a finished canvas, first trim off excess canvas around the edges, leaving about 3cm (1¼in) all around. Now, with the right sides facing, fold the corner diagonally towards the centre. Fold firmly and then press.

2 ♦ Fold the other two edges and stitch neatly along the diagonal seam. Secure all the edges on the back of the work with herringbone stitch, as shown.

Tent Stitch

*Tent stitch is the smallest needlepoint stitch
and also the most versatile and widely used. A diagonal
stitch, it is ideal for pictorial designs and complicated patterns as
well as smooth, plain areas of background. It is also
often used to frame other stitches.*

In use since the 14th century, if not before, tent stitch has been popular throughout needlework history. Also known as needle-point stitch, it is the stitch used in most surviving early pieces of needlepoint (not least because it is so durable). In Stuart times it was the main stitch used for covering caskets and jewel boxes with fine needlepoint, and it was also commonly used in the 19th century Berlin wool work, the first needlework done from printed charts.

Tent stitch is worked diagonally over only one intersection of the canvas. With this stitch, the needle always covers at least two threads on the wrong side of the work (unlike half cross stitch, a stitch which looks the same on the right side but covers only one thread on the wrong side, and which therefore distorts the canvas and is not very hardwearing). It is

because tent stitch covers two threads at the back that it is so durable. It can be worked on any type of canvas. Tent stitch can be worked in two different ways, known as basketweave (or diagonal) tent stitch and continental tent stitch. They look the same on the right side but on the wrong side are different.

Basketweave tent stitch, which is worked diagonally across the canvas, causes no distortion of the canvas because the stitches at the back are in a basketweave formation; this also makes it the more hardwearing of the two stitches. It is used principally for filling in motifs and backgrounds because of this.

Continental tent stitch, which is worked across the canvas from right to left and back again, has long, sloping stitches at the back. It is used mainly for outlining and fine detail but should not be used over large areas because of its distorting effect.

Stick with just one method when filling in large areas of one colour, especially for pale colours, so that the finished effect is uniform. If different methods are used, slight ridges and discrepancies may result even after the work has been stretched.

The most important thing to remember is to make sure the stitches always slant in the same direction. With this stitch, as long as the wool diagonally covers one intersection on the front of the work and at least two threads on the back, you can move wherever you want to, which is why it is so useful for intricate details and any form of pictorial design.

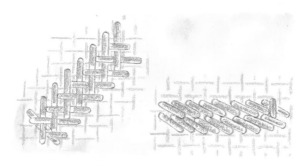

◆ *The reverse side of basketweave tent stitch (left) and continental tent stitch (right), showing their different construction*

BASKETWEAVE (DIAGONAL) TENT STITCH

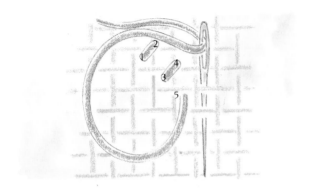

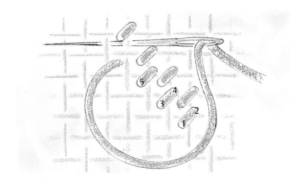

1 ◆ Starting at top left, and working diagonally down the canvas, make each stitch as follows. Bring needle out at 1 and take it over one intersection, inserting it at 2. Take it under two horizontal threads, bringing it out at 3. Continue in same way. Beneath last 'down' stitch in row, make one 'up' stitch.

2 ◆ Now work back up next line to fill in the spaces. For each stitch, bring needle out at 1 and diagonally over an intersection to upper right, inserting it at 2. Take it straight over to left across 2 vertical threads, bringing it out at 3. Continue in same way.

CONTINENTAL TENT STITCH

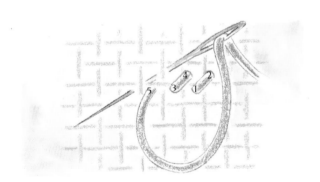

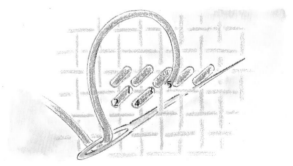

1 ◆ Starting at top right and working from right to left, make each stitch as follows. Bring needle out at 1 then take it diagonally over one intersection to upper right and insert it at 2. Take it diagonally across to lower left and bring it out at 3. Continue in same way along row. At end of row, finish with needle at back of canvas.

2 ◆ If you are holding the work, you can turn the canvas around and go back across the canvas parallel to the first row, again working from right to left. Alternatively, work back across row from left to right as shown. For each stitch, bring needle out at 1 and take it diagonally over one intersection to lower left, inserting it at 2. Take it diagonally across to upper right and bring it out at 3. Continue in same way.

BOXING CLEVER

*This pretty trinket box lid is stitched entirely in
tent stitch and shows how a fairly complicated design can be
achieved with one simple stitch. And being small,
it's an ideal project for starting out.*

SIZE

The lid is 9cm (3½in) in diameter.

STITCH USED

Continental tent (pages 14-15)

YOU WILL NEED

15cm (6in) × 15cm (6in) piece of 16 gauge single-thread canvas

Tapestry needle, size 20

1 skein each of the Paterna Persian wool listed with the chart (used as one thread)

Trinket box with 9cm (3½in) lid

Note: The trinket box used here (see page 72 for suppliers) is sent with everything necessary to assemble it easily. The backing disc supplied can be used as a template when drawing it out onto the canvas and when stretching the work.

PREPARATION

1 ◆ Roughly mark the centre of the canvas.

2 ◆ Using a permanent marker, draw a circle, 9cm (3½in) in diameter on the canvas, with the centre point of the circle at the centre of the canvas.

WORKING THE STITCHES

Following the chart shown opposite, work tent stitch from the centre outwards. If you find that one thread does not quite cover the canvas sufficiently, you may need to use two threads, but with most canvasses of this gauge, one thread will suffice.

FINISHING

1 ◆ Block and stretch the completed needlepoint.

2 ◆ When it is fully dry, place it in the lid to make sure that there is no bare canvas showing. If there is, simply add one or two stitches in the background red to cover it up. Work these stitches neatly as they won't be stretched.

3 ◆ Trim away excess canvas, leaving 6mm (¼in) of bare canvas all around the edge.

MAKING UP

To mount the canvas in the trinket box lid used here, first insert the piece of acetate then put in the completed needlepoint, followed by the paper disc and piece of foam. Push the locking plate in firmly, then stick on the flock lid liner using double-sided cellophane tape.

☑ 940 Cranberry
☐ 263 Off White
☑ D147 Basil
☑ 504 Federal Blue
☑ 691 Loden Green
☑ 652 Olive Green
☑ 662 Pine Green
☐ 523 Teal Blue

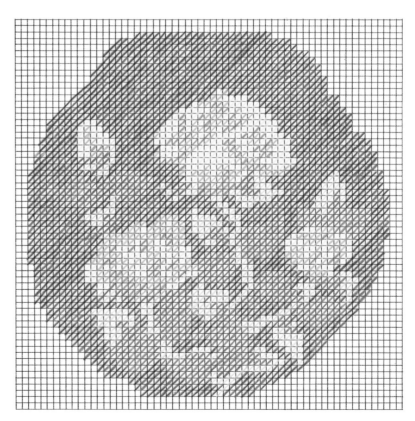

STRAIGHT GOBELIN STITCH

*This upright stitch is useful for filling large areas, for borders and
for all manner of patterns.*

Straight Gobelin stitch is one of the few surviving stitches from the Middle Ages. It takes its name from its resemblance to woven tapestries, such as those produced by the famous French factory at Gobelins, founded in 1450. Straight Gobelin stitch is one of the best-known of the straight stitches. Straight stitches in general are useful for pictorial work (although tent stitch is the most popular). They are quick because they can cover several threads at once, and they do not distort the canvas too much. Straight Gobelin stitches are all worked to the same vertical length in horizontal rows. They can be worked over any number of threads, but two, four and six are the most usual. For now, however, practise the stitch over just two threads, as this is used in the next project.

Encroaching straight Gobelin stitch is worked in a similar way but produces a different pattern because its rows overlap.

STRAIGHT GOBELIN STITCH	**ENCROACHING STRAIGHT GOBELIN STITCH**

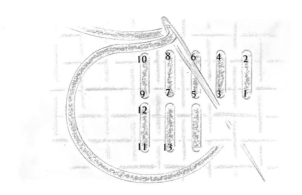

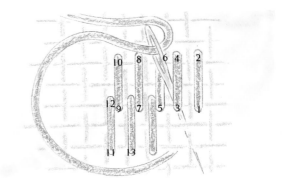

♦ Starting at upper right, bring needle out at 1, and insert it at 2; bring it out at 3. Continue in this way; at end of row reverse direction. Work back along row from left to right, sharing holes of previous row.

♦ Work first row as before, but work second row so tops are one horizontal thread above bases of previous row, and the stitches are consistently one thread to left or right of previous row.

BYZANTINE BOXES

This stitch sounds complicated yet is quick and easy. It makes an
attractive background filling stitch.

This stitch is a combination of continental tent stitch (see pages 14-15) and a bold diagonal stitch known as Byzantine stitch. Its name derives from the uniformly stepped zigzag pattern which was used in the art and textiles of the Byzantine Empire. Byzantine artists excelled at mosaic works, and a mosaic effect is apparent in this stitch, with its contrast between the long, slanting Byzantine stitches and the short tent stitches. Byzantine boxes are worked by first making the stepped outline of the boxes using tent stitch, then working Byzantine stitch between them and finally filling in the boxes with diagonal stitches.

BYZANTINE BOXES

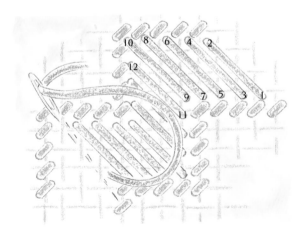

1 ◆ Make two diagonal stepped lines of continental tent stitch, working five stitches for each step (counting pivotal stitch twice). Now work **Byzantine stitch** over three intersections within tent stitch lines; alternate five horizontal and five vertical stitches (counting pivotal stitch twice) to form steps. Bring needle out at 1, insert it at 2, bring it out at 3 and so on.

2 ◆ Fill in the small boxes with diagonal stitches sloping in opposite direction to Byzantine stitches and covering one, then two, then three, then two and finally one canvas intersection.

Making your Mark

*Personalize your reading with this attractive bookmark,
which is quickly made using continental tent stitch, straight
Gobelin stitch and Byzantine boxes.*

SIZE

The bookmark measures
5.7cm (2¼in) × 24cm
(9½in).

STITCHES USED

Continental tent (pages
14-15), Straight Gobelin
(page 18), Byzantine boxes
(page 19)

YOU WILL NEED

33cm (13in) × 15cm (6in)
piece of 10 gauge double-
thread canvas

One skein each of Paterna
Persian wool listed with the
chart (used as whole, 3-ply
strands)

25cm (9¾in) × 7cm (2¾in)
piece of plain, stiff fabric
such as plain brocade

Thin cardboard (optional)

Thread (optional)

PREPARATION

Mark the outline of the bookmark
on your canvas – 22 threads across
and 95 down – centring it on the
piece of canvas you have cut.

WORKING THE STITCHES

1 ◆ Work the continental tent
stitch outline. Leave 2 threads
bare and work the inner tent
stitch outline, looking at the chart
as you work.
2 ◆ Next, work the continental
tent stitches that create the
Byzantine boxes. The direction
of the stitches is indicated on
the chart.
3 ◆ Work the Byzantine stitches
within the tent stitches, then fill
in the boxes with diagonal
stitches slanting in the opposite
direction to the Byzantine
stitches. These diagonal stitches
are also used in two places above
the Byzantine boxes.
4 ◆ Use straight Gobelin stitch to
fill in the area between the 2
framing rows of tent stitch, alternating the colours.

FINISHING

1 ◆ Block and stretch the completed needlepoint.
2 ◆ Trim away excess canvas, leaving 1.2cm (½in) of bare canvas all
around.
3 ◆ Neatly mitre the corners, and
catch down the raw canvas edges
on the wrong side with a few slip-
stitches.

MAKING UP

1 ◆ To make the fringe, cut 9cm
(3½in) lengths of each colour
wool, and hook different-coloured
lengths of wool through the holes
at one end of the bookmark, as
shown in the diagram. Use a fairly
fine crochet hook to do this,
inserting the hook with the right
side of the bookmark facing you.

◆ *Making the knotted fringe*

2 ◆ If you prefer a firm bookmark,
cut out thin cardboard using the
bookmark as your guide for the
size. Place the cardboard on the
wrong side of the work and turn
over the canvas edges, lacing
them together with thread from
top to bottom and from side to
side, mitring the corners. If you do
not want a firm bookmark, omit
this step.
3 ◆ Turn under the edges of the
piece of fabric so that it is exactly
the same size as the bookmark;

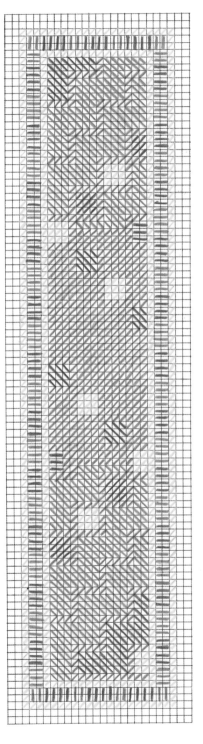

stitch the edges, then slip-stitch it to the back of the bookmark, pressing it neatly and carefully with a steam iron.

4 ◆ Trim the knotted fringe to an even length.

- ☐ 743 Tobacco
- ☑ 900 American Beauty
- ☑ 901 American Beauty
- ☑ 501 Federal Blue
- ☑ 502 Federal Blue
- ☑ 521 Teal Blue

CROSS STITCH

*The other main needlepoint stitch (along
with tent stitch), cross stitch is made up of a pair
of diagonally crossing stitches. It is an extremely useful stitch
for outlining, as a narrow border or for bold
lettering, and it is very hardwearing.*

Cross stitch is probably the oldest decorative stitch known. It has been found in needlework dating back to the 13th and 14th centuries and is still widely used in traditional needlework around the world to decorate folk costume and clothing as well as all kinds of household articles. Its hardwearing qualities have often led to its being the only stitch used in a piece of needlepoint, and it has always been used for church kneelers.

Cross stitch is worked over either one canvas intersection (as shown opposite) or two. The general rule is that the top diagonal stitches should all lie in the same direction, but if a deliberate difference in shade is desired, then the direction can be varied. You can work cross stitch in two stages, working a row of diagonals all sloping in the same direction and then working back along the row to complete the other diagonals. Alternatively, you can complete each stitch before doing the next. For borders, the first method is much quicker, while for small or very open motifs, it is easier to work complete stitches.

Not only is it possible to work cross stitch either in two stages or one stitch at a time but it can also be worked either vertically, horizontally or diagonally depending upon the design. Both single-thread and double-thread canvas are suitable.

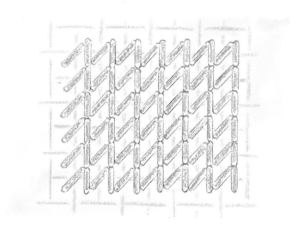

◆ *The reverse side of cross stitch worked one stitch at a time*

◆ *The reverse side of cross stitch worked in two stages*

CROSS STITCH WORKED ONE STITCH AT A TIME

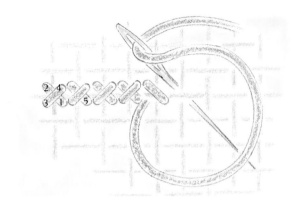

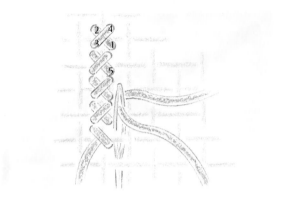

◆ To work horizontally, starting at upper left and working from left to right, make each stitch as follows. Bring needle out at 1, insert it at 2, bring it out at 3, insert it at 4, bring it out at 5 and continue in the same way. The next row is worked in reverse.

◆ To work vertically, starting at upper left and working from top to bottom, make each stitch as follows. Bring needle out at 1, insert it at 2, bring it out at 3, insert it at 4, bring it out at 5 and so on. At end of row, turn canvas and work in same way alongside first row.

CROSS STITCH WORKED IN TWO STAGES

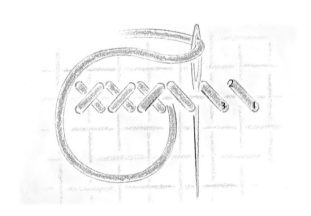

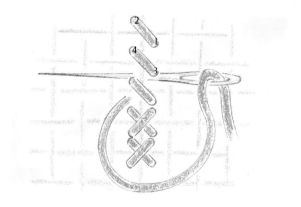

◆ To work horizontally, starting at upper right and working from right to left, make each stitch as follows. Bring needle out at 1, insert it at 2, bring it out at 3 and so on. Continue in same way to end of row, and then work back in reverse direction to form second diagonal on each stitch.

◆ To work vertically, starting at upper right and working from top to bottom, make each stitch as follows. Bring needle out at 1, insert it at 2, bring it out at 3 and so on. Continue in same way to end of row then work next row upwards in same way.

PRETTY AS A PICTURE

A picture frame like this lovely one worked
in continental tent stitch and cross stitch offers a
splendid chance to display your needlepoint skills. If you have a
particular picture in mind, you could alter some of
the colours to complement it. This would
also make a superb mirror frame.

SIZE

21.5cm (8½in) × 25cm (10in).

STITCHES USED

Continental tent (pages 14-15), Cross (pages 22-3)

SIZE

30.5cm (12in) × 35.5cm (14in) piece of 12 gauge interlock canvas

One skein each of the Paterna Persian wool listed with the chart (used as 2 threads)

Thin cardboard

Strong tape

PREPARATION

Find the centre of the canvas and mark it, using lines of running stitch or a permanent marker.

WORKING THE STITCHES

1 ◆ Stitch a rectangle of cross stitches around the centre, working 20 across the top and 30 down, as shown on the chart.
2 ◆ Leaving 14 threads outwards bare, work another rectangle of cross stitches. If you mark the thread that you are to work the cross stitches over before you start, then you will not have to keep stopping to count them.
3 ◆ When you have completed this second 'frame' of cross stitches, once again leave 14 threads bare all the way around, and then stitch the outermost rectangle of cross stitches.
4 ◆ Now you are ready to work the tent stitch as shown on the chart. Work the big flowers in the outermost frame corners first, then the inner frame corners and finally the smaller flowers and the background.

FINISHING

1 ◆ Block and then stretch the completed needlepoint before proceeding to make the frame, because once you have cut the canvas in the middle for the picture, you will not be able to stretch the work.
2 ◆ Trim away excess canvas to leave 2.5cm (1in) of bare canvas all around.
3 ◆ Cut diagonally across the corners, taking care not to cut too close to the fabric of the needlepoint itself.

☑	422 Coffee Brown
☑	310 Grape
☐	D521 Verdigris
☑	652 Olive Green
☐	743 Tobacco
☑	571 Navy Blue
☑	341 Periwinkle
☑	342 Periwinkle
☑	840 Salmon
☑	901 American Beauty
☑	311 Grape
☑	312 Grape
☑	912 Dusty Pink

MAKING UP

1 ◆ Cut 2 pieces of cardboard to the exact size of the needlepoint, cutting a hole in one to match the hole to be made for the picture.

2 ◆ To make the window in the middle of the canvas, cut the canvas in the centre and then carefully trim away the excess canvas to within 2.5cm (1in) of the stitching. Now cut diagonally into the corners as shown below.

3 ◆ With strong tape, reinforce the outer and inner canvas corners on the wrong side.

4 ◆ Place the cardboard with the cut-out hole over the back of the canvas, fold one long side over and tape it into place. Leave the remaining outer edges free. Now fold all the inner edges of the canvas over the cardboard, and tape them in place.

5 ◆ Place the second piece of cardboard on top of the first piece, fold the remaining outer edges of canvas back onto it and tape them to the cardboard. The picture can be inserted in the side with the open edge.

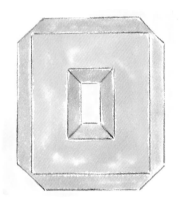

◆ *Placing one piece of cardboard over back of prepared canvas*

◆ *Folding inner edges and one outer edge of canvas back over cardboard*

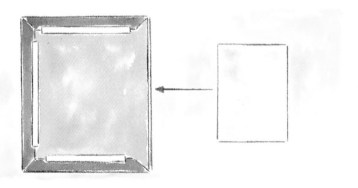

◆ *Sliding picture under second piece of cardboard through side with open edge*

Diagonal
Mosaic Stitch

Although this is a very simple stitch to master, it produces
interesting textural patterns.

Whereas most of the stitches covered so far have had a very long history, highly textured ones such as diagonal mosaic stitch, also known as condensed Scotch stitch, are a recent development. Until modern times, stitches were for the most part quite simple, because the astonishingly rich colours and intricate designs of the needlework provided enough interest. It was not really until the 20th century that diagonally patterned stitches such as this were used in profusion, especially in the 1950s and '60s. Traditionally, mosaic stitch consists of three diagonal stitches, which can be worked in various ways for particular textures. However, all manner of patterns can be worked by varying the scale and/or direction of the stitching.

DIAGONAL MOSAIC STITCH

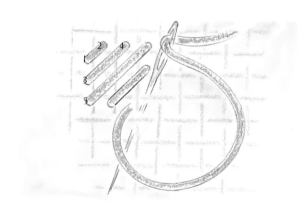

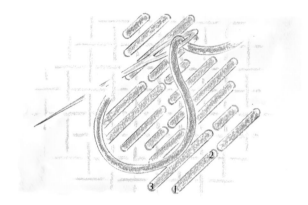

1 ◆ The first row is worked so that the stitches cover 3 intersections, then 2, then 1, then 2, then 3, and so on. Starting at upper left and working diagonally towards bottom right, bring needle out at 1, take it diagonally over to upper right and insert it at 2. Bring it out at 3, insert it at 4, out at 5, and so on.

2 ◆ Work back up next diagonal row, reversing procedure and working a stitch over just one intersection when it is adjacent to a 3-intersection stitch in previous diagonal row, and vice-versa. A 2-intersection stitch should be worked next to another 2-intersection stitch.

GRAND STAND

*Complete a festive tea table with this pretty
teapot stand worked in tent stitch and diagonal mosaic stitch.
The two shades of blue enhance the textural pattern
of this attractive background stitch.*

SIZE

The teapot stand is 12cm
(4¾in) in diameter.

STITCHES USED

Continental tent (pages 14-
15), Diagonal mosaic
(page 28)

YOU WILL NEED

18cm (7in) × 18cm (7in)
piece of 10 gauge double-
thread canvas

1 skein each of the Paterna
Persian wool listed with the
chart (used as 2 threads)

Double-sided tape

Teapot stand 11.5cm (4½in)
in diameter

Note: The teapot stand
used here (see page 72 for
suppliers) is sent with
everything necessary to
assemble it easily, including a self-adhesive felt base
and filler cards. The backing
disc which is supplied with
it can be used as a template
when stretching the work
and when drawing it out.

PREPARATION

1 ◆ Use the backing disc supplied
with the stand or make your own
template to the right size. Use this
to mark out a 12cm (4¾in) circle
in the centre of the canvas.

2 ◆ Centre the canvas over the
chart on page 30. You should then
be able to see the outlines of the
butterflies.

3 ◆ Using a permanent marker,
roughly mark the outlines of the
butterflies onto the canvas. You
will work from the chart but this is
useful as an additional guide.

4 ◆ Mark the top of your canvas
with an arrow so that you know
which way up you are working
each time you pick it up.

WORKING THE STITCHES

1 ◆ Work all the tent stitch areas
first before starting on the diagonal mosaic background.

2 ◆ Begin the diagonal mosaic
stitch at the upper left of your
work, choosing a part where the
mosaic is not broken up too much
by the butterflies, and then work
in that entire row.

3 ◆ The diagonal mosaic stitch is
worked as if the stitches were
carrying on behind the motifs, so

you stitch any parts of the pattern
that the butterflies do not
obscure. Where the butterflies
interrupt the diagonal flow of the
stitch, put in as much as is left of
the stitch. Follow on in this manner, working out as accurately as
you can where the mosaic will
come out.

FINISHING

1 ◆ Block and stretch the completed needlepoint, using your template as a guide. When it is
completely dry, place it in the
stand to make sure that there is
no bare canvas showing. If there
is, simply add one or two stitches
in the darker blue to cover it up.
Work these stitches neatly as they
won't be stretched.

2 ◆ Trim away excess canvas to
leave about 1.2cm (½in) of bare
canvas all around.

MAKING UP

1 ◆ Lay the teapot stand on the
underside of the self-adhesive felt
base and draw around the stand.
Cut to size.

2 ◆ Take one of the filler cards
included with the stand (or cut
your own) and hold it against the

back of the needlepoint to check that it will be flush with the back of the stand so that the canvas is pressed against the glass. If not, adjust the filler cards.

3 ◆ Fit the needlepoint into the frame of the stand, add the appropriate filler(s) and use double-sided tape to hold the work and card in place.

4 ◆ Remove the backing from the self-adhesive felt base provided with the kit, and stick the felt onto the back of the frame. The stand is now ready for use.

☑	☑	420/422	Coffee Brown
☑	☑	691/692	Loden Green
☑	☑	571/553	Navy/Ice Blue
	☑	930	Rusty Rose
	☑	833	Bittersweet
	☑	862	Copper
	☑	652	Olive Green
	☑	D511	Verdigris
	☑	743	Tobacco
	☐	465	Beige Brown
	☐	263	White
	☑	713	Mustard
	☑	210	Pearl Grey
	☑	341	Periwinkle
	☑	773	Sunny Yellow

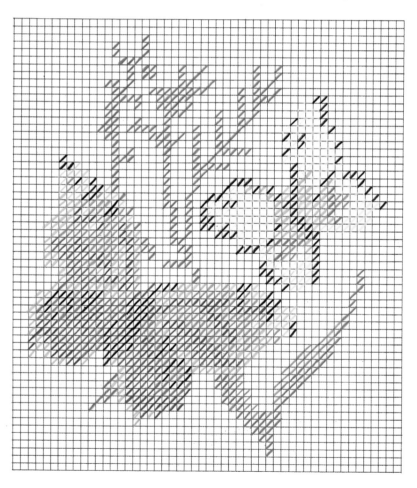

CUSHION STITCH

*Though rarely used in pictorial work, cushion stitch is excellent
for geometric patterns in one or more colours.*

Cushion stitch is traditionally used in 'stitchery' (a form of needlepoint using square, diamond-shaped and linear textured stitches to make geometric shapes that cover the canvas). Also known as Scotch stitch, it is made by working adjacent squares of five or seven parallel diagonal stitches, with the central one covering three or four intersections and the others graduating down to one. A variation, **chequer stitch**, has alternating squares of cushion stitch and basketweave tent stitch. It is used in the project on page 68, with seven diagonals for the cushion-stitch squares and 16 tent stitches (4 × 4) in the tent stitch squares.

CUSHION STITCH

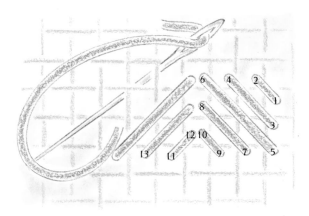

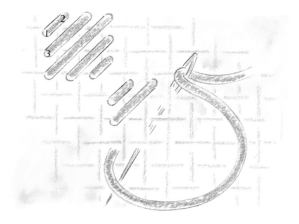

1 ◆ To produce a cushion stitch with five diagonals, you will cover first one, then two, then three, then two and finally one intersection. To work horizontally, starting at top right and working from right to left, bring needle out at 1, insert it at 2, bring it out at 3, and so on. For squares all sloping in the same direction, repeat on adjacent square. For opposite direction (as shown), work in reverse.

2 ◆ To work diagonally, starting at upper left and working from left to right, bring needle out at 1, insert it at 2, bring it out at 3 and so on. Miss one hole before starting second square. On last square in row, reverse direction and make another row of squares alongside first. This method is useful if you are working two colours in a chequerboard pattern and wish to work all the squares in one colour first.

MOSAIC AND REVERSED MOSAIC STITCHES

*Here are two more interesting variations on
the mosaic theme. They can be worked in different
colours to form many attractive geometric patterns and can also
be used as textured backgrounds, borders
or general filling stitches.*

These two stitches are similar to the last two stitches covered (diagonal mosaic stitch and cushion stitch). The mosaic stitch family gets its name from the patterns that can be built up using different colours for the squares, rather like mosaic work. Both stitches can be worked horizontally or diagonally, following much the same sequence as cushion stitch (see opposite). The difference is that whereas cushion stitch has five stitches per square (one long, flanked by two medium and two short), these two stitches have three: one medium, flanked by two short ones. The medium stitch covers two intersections, and the short ones cover one. As its name suggests, in reversed mosaic stitch each group of three diagonals is sloping in the opposite direction to the neighbouring groups of three. If you are working horizontally, you must reverse every other group of three diagonals. If you are working diagonally, however, all the stitches in each diagonal row slope the same way, while the adjacent rows slope in the opposite direction. Once you start doing reversed mosaic stitch, it's not nearly as complicated as it sounds!

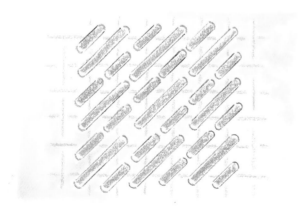

◆ Mosaic stitch, which is worked in the same way as cushion stitch but has only three diagonals per group

◆ Reversed mosaic stitch, which is worked like mosaic stitch but with alternating slopes for each group of three diagonals

FLOOR SHOW

*This decorative doorstop features no less than six
of the stitches you've learned — namely, tent, cushion,
straight Gobelin, cross, mosaic and reversed mosaic stitches.
If you prefer, you could substitute yarn colours to match
your room colour scheme or a nearby carpet.*

SIZE

The doorstop measures 22.5cm (8¾in) long × 11cm (4¼in) wide × 7.5cm (3in) high.

Note: If you cannot find a brick in the size specified, it is not difficult to adjust the needlepoint to fit the brick you use (for how to do this see instructions given under Preparation).

STITCHES USED

Continental tent (pages 14-15), Cushion (page 32), Straight Gobelin (page 18), Cross (pages 22-3), Reversed mosaic (page 33)

YOU WILL NEED

1 brick, 22cm (8⅝in) long × 10.5cm (4in) wide × 7cm (2¾in) high

45.5cm (18in) × 45.5cm (18in) piece of 10 gauge double-thread canvas

1 skein each of the Paterna Persian wool listed with the chart (used as 2 threads)

Interlining (optional)

48cm (19in) × 43cm (17in) piece of calico or similar fabric

25cm (9¾in) × 13.5cm (5¼in) piece of velvet or 22.5cm (8¾in) × 11cm (4¼in) piece of felt (for base)

Strong thread

Protective fabric treatment such as Scotchgard

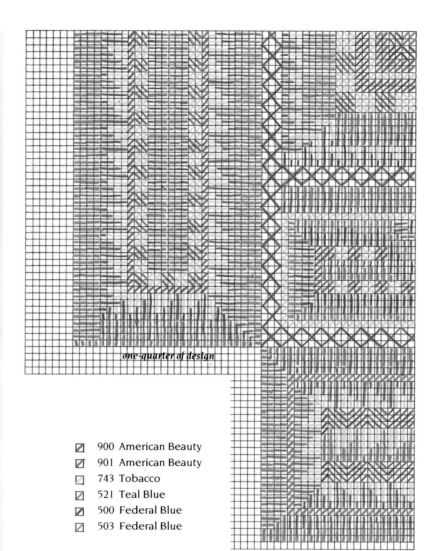

one-quarter of design

☑	900	American Beauty
☑	901	American Beauty
☐	743	Tobacco
☑	521	Teal Blue
☑	500	Federal Blue
☑	503	Federal Blue

PREPARATION

Mark the centre of the canvas. If your brick is a very different size, mark out the different measurements on your canvas and alter the chart as you work to fit the size of brick. If the brick is only slightly different, you can use the chart and leave out one row all the way around if it is smaller, or add an extra row if it is larger.

WORKING THE STITCHES

Work outwards from the centre, following the chart carefully. Only one-quarter of the design is shown, as the rest of the design is an exact mirror image of this. To follow the chart, turn the book through 90 degrees as you complete each quarter of the design. Its symmetry makes it easy to work.

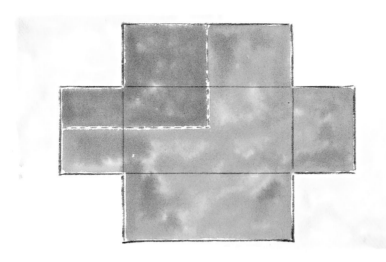

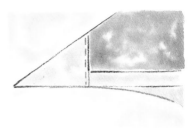

◆ Sewing corners of worked canvas together, with right sides facing

◆ Diagram of completed needlepoint (shaded area indicates portion covered by chart)

FINISHING
Block and stretch the completed needlepoint.

MAKING UP
1 ◆ If your brick has a dip in it, fill this out with interlining to give a level surface.
2 ◆ To prevent the canvas from being damaged by the rough edges of the brick and ensure a snug fit of the needlepoint around the brick, cover the whole brick with calico. Wrap it up as you would a parcel and neatly sew down all the sides, trimming off the excess as you go to give a good crisp outline.
3 ◆ Fold the needlepoint with right sides together, and firmly stitch each corner by hand with strong thread as near to the needlepoint as possible, but not through the stitches themselves.
4 ◆ Trim away excess canvas, leaving about 1.2cm (½in) seam allowances. Open the trimmed

seams and run your fingernail along them.
5 ◆ Use herringbone stitch (see page 13) to sew down the seam allowances to the back of the work. Repeat for other sides.
6 ◆ Turn the work right side out and place it over the brick, pulling it firmly to give a snug fit.
7 ◆ Lace the lower edges of the canvas together across the base of the brick from top to bottom and from side to side, pulling the canvas taut as you go.
8 ◆ If you are using velvet, turn under 1.2cm (½in) all around, and stitch in place. The velvet or felt should be the exact size of the base of the brick. Slip-stitch this over the lacing, taking in canvas threads rather than needlepoint as you proceed.
9 ◆ As the doorstop will receive a great deal of wear and tear, spray the needlepoint with fabric protector, after first testing for colour fastness.

◆ Cutting away excess canvas from seam allowance at each corner

◆ Sewing down seam allowances to back of work using herringbone stitch

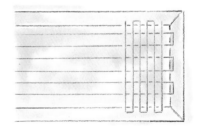

◆ Lacing lower edges of canvas together over bottom of brick

WEB STITCH

Another interesting textural filling stitch,
web stitch gives a firm, woven texture. It can be
worked in one or two colours, but two is more usual. It is
particularly effective for leaves, textured borders and
other patterned work.

Web stitch is sometimes stitched by first laying down long diagonal threads across the canvas and then catching them down with alternate long diagonal threads, which are usually in a second colour. It is more usual, however, to work web stitch in the way shown here, and as each stitch is done individually, this method is more versatile.

With web stitch, the stitches of each row fit neatly against the previous row, with the diagonals sloping in alternate directions. Whereas on the front of the canvas all the stitches are diagonal, on the back all the stitches are upright, in staggered rows. When working this stitch, be sure to use a thick-enough yarn to cover the canvas well and give a firm texture.

WEB STITCH

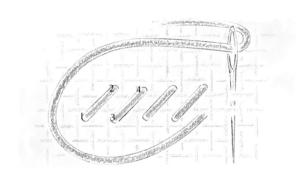

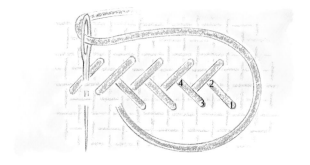

1 ◆ Working horizontally from left to right, make a row of diagonal stitches, bringing needle out at 1, taking it diagonally to upper right over two canvas intersections and inserting it at 2. Bring it out again at 3 and continue in this way along row. On the back there will be a row of vertical stitches.

2 ◆ Working next row horizontally right to left, with second colour (if using), bring needle out at 1, take it diagonally to upper left over two canvas intersections and insert it at 2. Bring it out at 3 and continue in the same way along the row. Carry on working back and forth row by row.

Hungarian Stitch

*Hungarian stitch is a straight stitch that is useful
as a filling and background stitch. It is particularly good
for shading an area gradually, because it can be
blended in bands, as in the next project.*

This stitch produces a smooth, but attractive pattern of small diamonds, creating an almost heraldic effect, particularly when worked in two colours. In pictorial designs it is useful for anything from diamond-paned windows and roof tiles to lawns and fields. The actual stitches are simple to do but care is needed when forming the patterns. Hungarian stitch consists of groups of three upright stitches – a long one (covering four threads) with a short one (covering two threads) on each side; the groups are separated by gaps of two vertical threads. The stitches are worked from side to side, with the rows interlocking so the tall stitches fit into the gaps in the previous row. You can work all the rows in one colour, or every row in a different colour.

HUNGARIAN STITCH

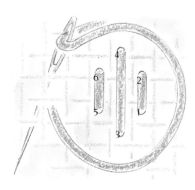

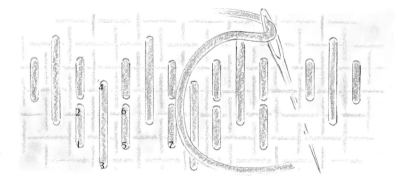

1 ◆ Starting at top right and working from right to left for first row, bring needle out at 1 and insert it at 2. Bring it out at 3, and insert it at 4. Bring it out at 5, and insert it at 6. You now have a group of three upright stitches: one long one flanked by two short ones. Skip one hole (ie, two threads) and repeat. Continue to end of row.

2 ◆ At end of row, reverse direction so you are working from left to right. Bring needle out at 1 and insert it at 2. Bring it out at 3 and insert it at 4. Bring it out at 5 and insert it at 6. Continue in same way. Carry on working back and forth row by row.

Say it with Flowers

*Longer-lasting than most flowers, this unusual
greetings card is a gift in itself and likely to become
a treasured keepsake. It's made with tent, straight Gobelin,
web and Hungarian stitches. A lot of colours have been used
but some are also required for other projects in this book,
and a good range of colours is never wasted.*

SIZE

The needlepoint portion measures 13cm (5in) in diameter, and the card measures 22.9cm (9in) × 19.5cm (7¾in).

STITCHES USED

Continental tent (pages 14-15), Straight Gobelin (page 18), Web (page 37), Hungarian (page 38)

YOU WILL NEED

23cm (9in) × 23cm (9in) piece of 12 gauge interlock canvas

1 skein each of the Paterna Persian wool listed with the chart (used as 2 threads)

Thin, coloured cardboard or painted thick watercolour paper

Double-sided tape

Strong glue

Paper glue

PREPARATION

1 ◆ Mark the centre of the canvas.
2 ◆ Draw a 13cm (5in) circle around this centre point using a permanent marker.

WORKING THE STITCHES

1 ◆ Following the chart on page 40, work tulips and stems in tent stitch.
2 ◆ Only the tulips are shown on the chart because it is simpler to work the rest of the design by following the photograph. Stitch the background in Hungarian stitch, working outwards from the tulips until you reach the border.
3 ◆ Work the lighter leaves in straight Gobelin stitch, and the darker ones in web stitch.

FINISHING

1 ◆ Block and stretch the completed needlepoint by making a 13cm (5in) round template and stretching the canvas out to make an even, circular piece of work.
2 ◆ Trim away excess canvas, leaving 1.2cm (½in) of bare canvas all around.

MAKING UP

1 ◆ In some craft shops you can purchase cards in which to place your needlepoint. Otherwise, you can make your own from thin cardboard or thick watercolour paper. Cut out a 45.7 cm (18in) × 19.5cm (7¾in) piece. Score the halfway line (along the long dimension) with your fingernail, then fold it in half along this line.
2 ◆ With the folded edge on your left, use a compass to draw a 13cm (5in) circle on the front. Cut this out.
3 ◆ Centre the needlepoint in the cut-out window and fasten it with double-sided tape. When you are happy with the position of the needlepoint, tape it down firmly with strong tape.
4 ◆ Cut a further piece of cardboard measuring 19.5cm (7¾in) × 22.9cm (9in). Glue the second piece of cardboard over the wrong side of the needlepoint to line up with the edges of the front of the greetings card.
5 ◆ Press the card under something heavy to give it a crisp look.

☐ 772 Sunny Yellow
◩ 823 Tangerine
◩ 970 Christmas Red
◩ 571 Navy Blue
◩ 940 Cranberry
◩ 653 Olive Green
◩ 900 American Beauty
◩ 311 Grape
◩ 652 Olive Green
◩ 843 Salmon
☐ 263 Cream
☐ 260 White
◩ 313 Grape
◩ 846 Salmon
◩ 334 Lavender
◩ 855 Spice
◩ 522 Teal Blue

Outer Circle
◩ D516 Ocean Green
◩ 692 Loden Green
☐ 694 Loden Green
◩ 691 Loden Green

Background
☐ 555 Ice Blue
◩ 342 Periwinkle
◩ 503 Federal Blue

LONG AND SHORT STITCH

This stitch makes a delightful background or filling stitch and lends itself well to delicate shading in bands of colour. It also forms a good outlining stitch.

This stitch is not difficult to work but it does require careful placement. It consists of alternate long and short stitches arranged so that pairs of rows interlock, with the short stitches from one row adjacent to the long stitches of the other row. Yarns in graduating tones from dark to light are generally used. The long and short stitches are worked over, say, six and four threads respectively, or four and two threads. They should never be too long, as the loops can easily get caught. Long and short stitch can also be worked in curves. Make the first stitch on the centre of the curve, then work down each side, angling the stitches to fit.

LONG AND SHORT STITCH

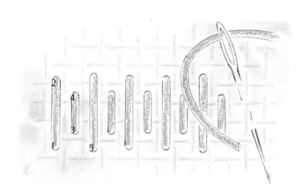

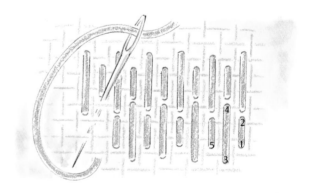

1 ◆ Starting at top left and working from left to right, bring needle out at 1, take it vertically over, say, four threads and insert it at 2. Bring it out at 3, take it vertically over, say, two threads and insert it at 4. Bring it out at 5, and continue in same way to end of row.

2 ◆ Using a second colour and working from right to left, bring needle out at 1 and insert it at 2, bring it out at 3 and insert it at 4, and so on. The stitches should cover the same number of horizontal threads as the first row but long ones are next to short ones, and vice-versa. They share holes where they adjoin.

CUSHION STITCH VARIATION

*Worked in two or more colours, cushion stitch variation
makes a lovely border, and is also useful as a background,
creating attractive effects of light and shade.*

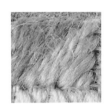

This variation of cushion stitch (see page 32) has two central diagonals (covering four intersections each) rather than one as in cushion stitch itself, and is worked in alternating colours for each rectangular 'cushion'. It is easiest to keep the different-coloured yarns going at the same time on separate needles, so that you complete each cushion before going on to the next. Because the diagonals of each cushion slope in the opposite direction to those of the adjacent cushions, the light catches them differently, giving quite complex effects, particularly when subtly different shades of yarn are used for the cushions.

CUSHION STITCH VARIATION

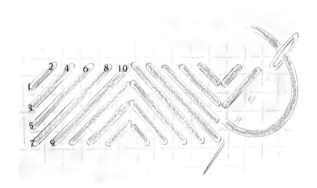

1 ◆ Cushion stitch variation has eight diagonals, covering first one intersection, then two, then three, then four, then four again, then three, then two and finally one intersection, creating a rectangular shape measuring five threads by six threads. Bring needle out at 1, insert it at 2, bring it out at 3 and so on.

2 ◆ Adjacent squares slope in the opposite direction, creating interesting textures. If you wish to work another row alongside the first row, reverse direction at end of row.

PICTURE THIS

This lovely poppies needlepoint picture is loosely
based on a painting by a Japanese artist, Togyu Okumara, who
was born at the end of the 19th century.

SIZE

The picture measures 39cm (15¼in) × 21cm (8¼in).

STITCHES USED

Continental tent (pages 14-15), Long and short (page 42), Cushion stitch variation (page 43)

YOU WILL NEED

48cm (19in) × 30.5cm (12in) piece of 10 gauge double-thread canvas

1 skein each of the Paterna Persian wool listed with the chart (used as 2 threads)

Cardboard

Strong thread

Picture frame or 51cm (20in) × 33cm (13in) piece of backing fabric such as plain brocade, velvet, heavy linen, twill or rep

PREPARATION

1 ♦ Mark out an area 38cm (13in) × 20.5cm (8in) in the centre of your canvas with a marker pen.

2 ♦ Mark the central threads on your canvas within this area, then mark the border. Now roughly mark the outlines of the poppies and leaves.

WORKING THE STITCHES

1 ♦ Following the chart on pages 46-7, work the poppies and leaves in tent stitch.

2 ♦ The background is worked in long and short stitch in 2 shades ot beige. Work the darker shade around the poppies and leaves; it should be worked to a depth of one stitch all the way around the motifs. Then work the lighter shade to bring the background out to the edge of your marked area

3 ♦ Use the same 2 shades of beige for the border. Work cushion stitch variation across the top and bottom border, then down each side. The border is 160 threads × 84 threads, so 14 of the 6-thread-wide cushions will fit exactly across the top and bottom, and 25 down the remaining border on each side.

FINISHING

1 ♦ Block and stretch the completed needlepoint.

2 ♦ Trim away excess canvas to leave about 1.2cm (½in) of bare canvas all around.

MAKING UP

1 ♦ To back the panel, cut a piece of cardboard the exact size of the finished panel. If you plan to back the panel with fabric, use thin cardboard. If you plan to frame it with a purchased picture frame, use thicker cardboard.

2 ♦ Place the cardboard against the wrong side of the work, and fold the raw edges of the canvas over the top of the cardboard.

3 ♦ Using strong thread, lace the raw edges together over the cardboard from top to bottom and from side to side.

4 ♦ Now either frame the panel or back it with fabric. If you frame it, remember that needlepoint pictures should be framed without glass to allow the texture of the stitches to be fully appreciated. To back it, turn under about 1.2cm (½in) all around the backing fabric so that it is exactly the size of the finished panel, and stitch. Slip-stitch the fabric neatly to the back of the panel, then sew 2 curtain rings to the top corners so it is ready to hang.

top

	261 Cream	☑	621 Shamrock	☑	913 Dusty Pink	☑	D502 Seafarer
☑	523 Teal Blue	☑	351 Fuchsia	☑	435 Chocolate Brown	☑	521 Teal Blue
☑	662 Pine Green	☑	900 American Beauty	☑	644 Khaki Green	☑	915 Dusty Pink

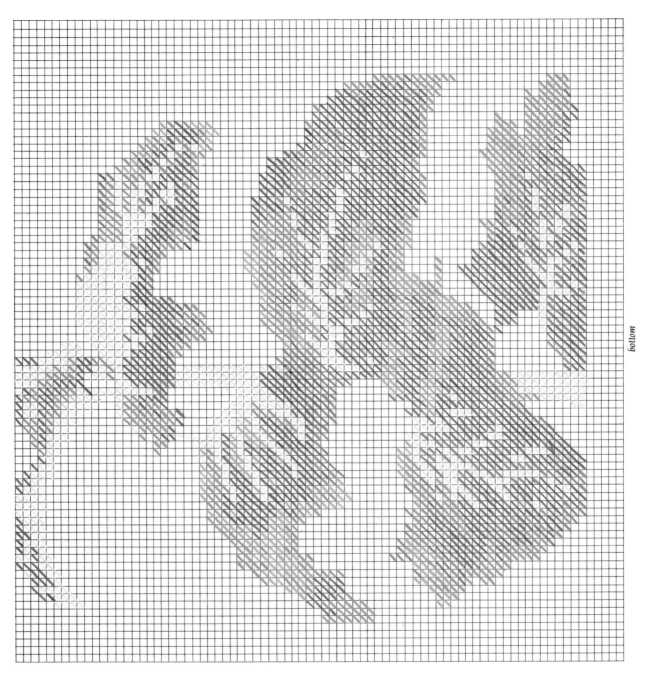

bottom

☑	840 Salmon	☑	353 Fuchsia
☑	313 Grape	☑	844 Salmon
☑	433 Chocolate Brown	☐	964 Hot Pink

FLORENTINE WORK

*Relatively simple to work and producing
quick-growing, dramatic-looking results, Florentine
stitching, which is also known as Bargello work, is deservedly
popular. Patterns can be large or small,
simple or sophisticated.*

Whole books have been written just on the subject of Florentine work. So many lovely patterns and effects are possible that it forms a complete branch of needlepoint in its own right. Florentine work goes back to at least the 16th century in Renaissance Italy. It enjoyed a revival in the 18th century, when needle-workers on both sides of the Atlantic stitched it in wool for upholstery and in silks for smaller items.

Although Florentine work is actually defined as any design worked on canvas with straight stitches, tradi-tionally it means a unique form of stitching in which Florentine stitch or any of its variations is used to produce recognizable zigzag patterns. The alternate peaks and valleys in all of the stitches of Florentine work are made up of straight Gobelin stitches (see page 18) arranged to form diagonal patterns through the use of 'steps' up or down between the stitches.

Most patterns are started in the centre of the canvas. The first row, or pattern row, is worked from the centre outwards. Subsequent rows may be worked above or below it but they always follow this original row, and are worked from side to side. Florentine stitch can be anywhere from two to eight stitches tall but is generally worked over four to six threads.

Curves are created by working blocks of stitches the same height next to each other. Mirror image patterns are also used, in which the top and bottom pattern mirror each other, or the pattern is symmetri-cal in four directions.

Apart from the distinctive pattern, colour is the other most notable feature of Florentine work, adding depth and movement to the pattern. Traditionally, the patterns shade gradually from light into dark and back, combining several different tones of each of two or three basic colours for lovely, subtle effects. However, more striking colour combinations are also used. When experimenting with colours, remember that the zigzag line will be most distinct if you start with a dark shade and graduate to lighter ones.

The simplest pattern is the basic Florentine stitch itself, in which the peaks and valleys are all the same depth. Combinations of pointed peaks and valleys of different sizes are known as flame stitch; there is no set pattern for this. Hungarian point is another stitch used; a variation of this is shown opposite.

Most Florentine charts are line charts (see page 12). A standard way of describing stitches in Floren-tine work is with a number such as 4.2, which means a stitch length of 4 (ie, it crosses 4 horizontal threads) and a step of 2 (the number of horizontal threads between the bases of adjacent stitches).

Single-thread canvas gives the best results. Make sure your yarn is thick enough to cover the canvas – straight stitches don't cover quite so well as diagonal ones, so you may need thicker yarn than usual if you are used to working, say, tent stitch. Don't skimp on yarn by not working in the proper 'over and over' sequence, as the stitches will not lie flat.

FLORENTINE STITCH

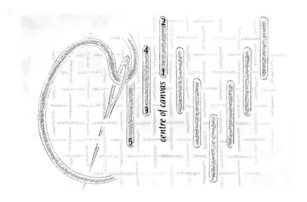

1 ◆ Here the stitch length is four and the step is two. Start first row in centre and work out to left and right. Always work 'over and over', bringing needle out at 1 and inserting it at 2, out at 3 and so on.

2 ◆ All the other rows follow this pattern row but start at either the left or the right, rather than the centre. They may be worked above or below the pattern row.

HUNGARIAN POINT VARIATION

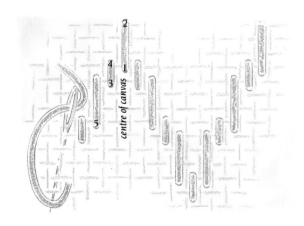

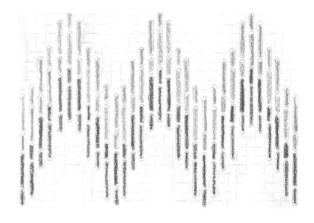

1 ◆ Begin with pattern row: start it in centre and work out to left and right. Each row consists of alternating long straight stitches (over four canvas threads) and short straight ones (over two canvas threads) with alternating steps of one and three. Bring needle out at 1, insert it at 2, out at 3 and so on.

2 ◆ In even-numbered rows of this stitch, the straight stitches are in reverse order, so that short stitches in one row butt up to long stitches in adjacent rows, and all the adjoining rows fit neatly together.

COMING TO FRUITION

*Iridescent colours, textural
stitches and luscious fruit motifs make this
place mat wonderfully exotic, while the zigzag patterns of the
Byzantine boxes in the background and the Florentine
border add to the rich appearance.*

SIZE

The place mat measures
35.5cm (14in) × 28cm (11in).

STITCHES USED

Continental Tent (pages
14-15), Straight Gobelin
(page 18), Byzantine boxes
(page 19), Hungarian point
variation (page 49)

YOU WILL NEED

45.5cm (18in) × 38cm (15in)
piece of 10 gauge double-
thread canvas

1 skein each of the Paterna
Persian wool listed with the
chart (used as 3 threads)

35.5cm (14in) × 28cm (11in)
piece of felt or other heat-
absorbing fabric
(optional)

Thin sheet of cork
(optional)

Fabric protector such as
Scotchgard

Matching thread

PREPARATION

1 ◆ Enlarge the chart shown on
pages 52-3 by 131% on a photocopier and then mark the outer
perimeter of the needlepoint.
Alternatively, by placing the canvas over the enlarged chart mark
the outer perimeter by measuring
35.5cm (14in) × 28cm (11in) and
centring this area on your canvas.
Now mark the border by counting
in 10 *holes* and marking the next
thread. Find the point at which
you wish to begin and, following
the chart, work from there.
2 ◆ Draw the outlines of the subjects onto the canvas. Using the
outlines and the chart you will be
able to copy the design.

WORKING THE STITCHES

1 ◆ Work all the subjects first,
because it is much easier to put
the background in around them,
and you can see the outlines you
want to achieve for the fruit more
easily.
2 ◆ When you have completed the
subjects, work in the tent stitching for the Byzantine boxes. If you
find it too difficult to work out
exactly where the boxes will come
out on the other side of the fruit
or leaves, use a ruler and roughly
mark in where you think it will
come out. As long as it looks as if
the boxes are spaced out evenly
when the place mat is finished, it
does not matter if it is not correct
to the nearest thread.
3 ◆ Finish the stitching on the
same thread on each side so that
you have a straight side on each
edge of the place mat and the
border is even.
4 ◆ Find the exact centre of the
bottom edge and then follow the
chart to work the mirror image in
the corners.
5 ◆ Work out from the centre of
the top of the place mat in the
same way, following the chart to
make the corners fit. Then follow
on down the sides in the same
way until you reach the mirror
image that you have just stitched
on the bottom corner.

FINISHING

Block and stretch the completed
needlepoint.

MAKING UP

1 ◆ It would be a good idea to use a fabric protector such as Scotch-gard on the surface of the needle-point in case of spillages.

2 ◆ It is also a good idea to back the mat with a heat-absorbent fabric like felt. (If you wish, you could put a thin layer of cork between the needlepoint and the backing fabric too.) Cut a piece of felt to the dimensions of the canvas. Press down the canvas across the corners of the needle-point with a steam iron. Next, fold the canvas on both sides of each corner and bring the edges together to form a neat diagonal seam on the wrong side, then press again. Sew this down with herringbone stitch (see page 13).

3 ◆ Sew the felt down neatly on the back of the needlepoint using small stitches and picking up threads of canvas rather than needlepoint stitches.

- 341 Periwinkle
- 541 Cobalt Blue
- 692 Loden Green
- 662 Pine Green
- 652 Olive Green
- D516 Ocean Green
- 863 Copper
- 834 Bittersweet
- 310 Grape
- 311 Grape
- 312 Grape
- 313 Grape
- 951 Strawberry
- 952 Strawberry
- 704 Butterscotch
- 962 Hot Pink
- 840 Salmon

VELVET STITCH

*Based on cross stitch, this lovely stitch is an example
of a loop, or pile, stitch, in which loops of yarn formed by the
stitches create a pile on the surface of the canvas.*

Used in embroidery as well as needlepoint, velvet stitch was first seen in the reign of Charles I and was again widely used in the 18th century in Savonnerie tapestries. It became very popular in the 19th century, when Victorian tufting, or plush work, was used. The main work was in a flat stitch like tent stitch. with velvet stitch used for areas requiring high relief, such as flowers, fur and feathers. Velvet stitch can be worked over two threads of single canvas or over one or two (double) threads of double canvas. Worked over one thread, it resembles bouclé yarn. Practise it over two threads first. The loops may be cut or left uncut.

VELVET STITCH

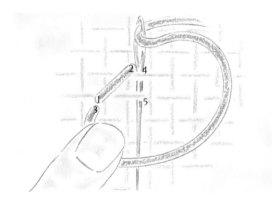

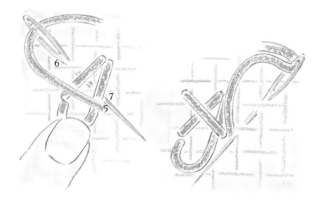

1 ◆ Starting at lower left and working from left to right, make each stitch as follows. Bring needle out at 1, take it to upper right over two canvas intersections and insert it at 2. Take it to lower left under two intersections and bring it out at 3 (same hole as 1). Take it over to 4 (same hole as 2), leaving a small loop of yarn, which you hold with your left index finger. Bring it out at 5, with point of needle under loop.

2 ◆ Take needle diagonally over two intersections to upper left and insert it at 6. Bring needle out at 7 (same hole as 5) and repeat. Begin new row at left. These diagrams show velvet stitch worked over two threads of single canvas, but the same technique can be used when working it over one or two (double) threads of double canvas.

SMYRNA STITCH

*Another stitch based on cross stitch, Smyrna
stitch forms a square, raised stitch that is traditionally used in the
geometric patterns of stitchery.*

Although Smyrna stitch is seen most often in the textural work of the 1950s and '60s, it had a brief period of great popularity in the Victorian era, often embellished with beads. Smyrna stitch may be worked over two threads (as in the next project), three threads (as the Victorians did) or four threads. It is formed by

working a basic cross stitch and then an upright cross stitch over the top. Smyrna stitch may be worked in a single colour, or you can do complete stitches in alternating colours for a chequerboard pattern. For a different effect the base cross can be worked in one colour and the top one in another.

SMYRNA STITCH

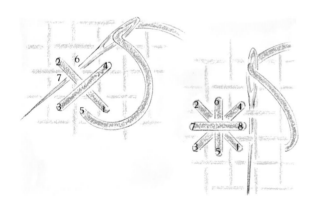

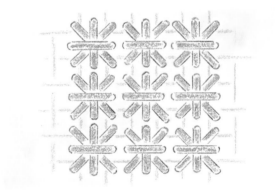

1 ◆ Starting at upper left and working from left to right, make each stitch as follows. Bring needle out at 1, and insert it at 2. Bring it out at 3 and insert it at 4. You now have the basic cross. Bring it out at 5 and insert it at 6. Bring it out at 7 and insert it at 8. You now have an upright cross stitch on top of the basic cross stitch. Always follow the same sequence so that all the stitches finish with the same stitch.

2 ◆ Continue in same way to end of row, then work back from right to left beneath first row. Top holes of new row should be same as bottom holes of previous row.

WOOLLY THINKING

*The contrast between the ewe and
lamb's woolly coats, worked in velvet stitch, and
their legs and faces, done in tent stitch, adds to the charm of this
landscape picture. A two-tone Smyrna stitch border
provides further textural interest.*

SIZE

The needlepoint picture, without the frame, measures 23cm (9in) × 20.5cm (8in).

STITCHES USED

Continental tent (pages 14-15), Velvet (page 54), Smyrna (page 55)

YOU WILL NEED

33cm (13in) × 30.5cm (12in) piece of 12 gauge interlock canvas

One skein each of the Paterna Persian wool listed with the chart (used as 2 threads)

Cardboard

Piece of dark brocade fabric at least 40.5cm (16in) × 38cm (15in)

Thread

Tape

Glue (optional)

PREPARATION

1 ◆ Mark out on the centre of your canvas a rectangle measuring 23cm (9in) × 20.5cm (8in).
2 ◆ Enlarge the chart by 120% and place under canvas, to mark out the ewe and lamb, the areas of shadow and the line of the horizon.

WORKING THE STITCHES

1 ◆ Referring to the chart, stitch in the ewe and lamb, working each one's body and a little of the neck in velvet stitch and the legs and face in tent stitch. Don't worry if you cannot manage velvet stitch in every single hole. As you work the sheep, it gets crowded and it will look as if every hole has been worked.
2 ◆ The velvet stitch takes quite a long time to work, so when the sheep are finished, you can speedily do the landscape and sky in tent stitch.
3 ◆ Finish the piece of work by stitching a border in Smyrna stitch, using the two shades indicated on the chart.

FINISHING

Block and stretch the completed needlepoint.

MAKING UP

1 ◆ The dark fabric can be used to frame the needlepoint directly. First mitre the corners of the canvas (see page 13).
2 ◆ Press the back of the needlepoint with a steam iron to give a neat finish to all the edges.
3 ◆ For a 4cm (1½in) frame all around, cut a 30.5cm (12in) × 28cm (11in) piece of cardboard (or larger if a deeper frame is required). Cut out a window in the centre for the worked canvas.

☐	213 Pearl Grey
▨	D389 Dolphin
☐	515 Old Blue
▨	514 Old Blue
☐	263 Cream
☐	465 Beige Brown
▨	652 Olive Green
☐	653 Olive Green
▨	641 Khaki Green
▨	221 Charcoal
▨	D511 Verdigris

◆ *Placing cardboard 'frame' on fabric that will cover it*

4 ◆ Place the cardboard frame on the wrong side of your fabric. Adding 3.5cm (1¼in) all around the outer edge and 2cm (¾in) all around the inner edge, mark and cut out the fabric 'frame'.

5 ◆ Turn under 1.2cm (½in) on all outer corners of the fabric; press.

6 ◆ Place the cardboard back on the wrong side of the fabric. Cut the fabric along the diagonals from the inner corners to the cardboard inner corners. Fold the fabric back along each inner edge, stretching it fairly taut, and tape it to the cupboard.

7 ◆ Mitre the fabric at one of the outer corners (see page 13) but do not sew it yet. Press across the diagonal edge. Repeat for the three other corners. Now glue or sew the diagonal seam at each corner.

8 ◆ Slip-stitch the needlepoint onto the fabric at the back of the frame.

9 ◆ Cut a further piece of cardboard to the size of the framed needlepoint, and tape to back.

STRAIGHT STITCHES

*Straight stitches, which are worked to
lie parallel to the canvas threads (usually the vertical threads),
are very versatile and can produce many
interesting patterns and effects.*

Straight stitches have been used for centuries. They can be seen in early samplers and many pieces of 17th century needlework. You have already learned decorative ways of using several straight stitches, but many other effects are also possible, as can be seen in the next project. Try experimenting with the variations shown below and with your own combinations of straight stitches and colours.

Using straight stitches in a fairly uniform way produces a textile that is close and hard-wearing.

Straight stitches that are fairly long are less durable, however, as the long stitches can loosen with wear. Another advantage is that they tend not to pull and distort the canvas as much as diagonal stitches do. With their clean areas of colour, straight stitches are often used for certain areas in pictorial work, particularly as random long stitch. Subtle gradations of colour, as in Florentine work, are also possible. Straight stitches can be worked horizontally or vertically, in small groups or in rows, in patterns or at random.

STRAIGHT STITCH VARIATIONS

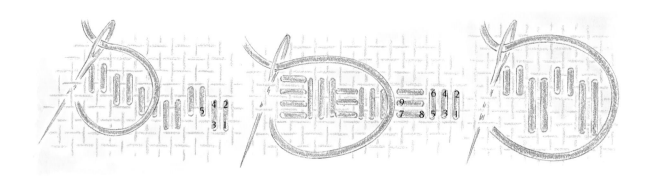

◆ Instead of working straight stitches side by side, which is obviously the more usual way, you could try staggering the groups of stitches, as in the simple step variation shown in the diagram on the left above.

In the middle diagram above, alternate blocks have simply been worked horizontally instead of vertically. The diagram above illustrates how stitches of different lengths can be used to make interesting patterns.

LONG STITCH

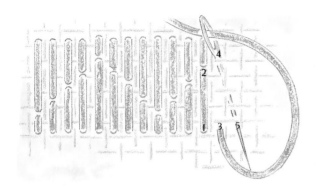

♦ Long stitch is particularly useful for patterned areas. Each stitch is worked over one, then two, three, four, five, four, three and finally two threads. The stitches in the second row are worked over five, then four, three, two, one, two, three and four threads, and share holes with those in the previous row. All rows are worked from left to right. Work 'over and over' as shown so stitches lie flat.

PARISIAN STITCH

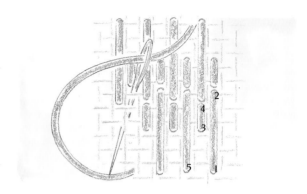

♦ In this popular background or filling stitch, short and long stitches alternate. The short stitches of one row share holes with the long stitches of adjacent rows and vice-versa, so that the rows interlock. Parisian stitch may be worked over six and two threads, as here, or four and two, or three and one. The rows are worked alternately from left to right, and from right to left.

BRICK STITCH

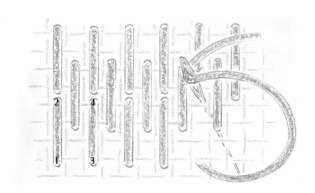

♦ A useful filling stitch which is good for shading, brick stitch is worked over two, four or sometimes six threads. All the stitches are of the same length, but alternate stitches begin halfway up from the first stitch. Rows are worked right to left, then left to right.

RANDOM LONG STITCH

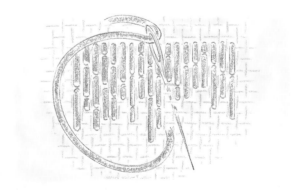

♦ Random long stitch, which is ideal for filling large areas of canvas quickly, is worked in varying lengths along each row. It is worked row by row, alternately from left to right then from right to left, with the rows interlocking.

VARIATIONS ON A THEME

*Made entirely with variations of straight stitch,
this very rich, Eastern-looking cushion is a perfect example
of the wealth of diverse effects that can be
created by experimentation.*

SIZE

The cushion measures 39cm
(15½in) × 39cm (15½in).

STITCHES USED

Variations of straight stitch
(page 60)

YOU WILL NEED

48cm (19in) × 48cm (19in)
piece of 10 gauge double-
thread canvas

One skein each of the
Paterna Persian wool listed
with the chart (used as complete strands)

Approximately 50cm (½yd)
of backing fabric such as
velvet (used here), bro-
cade, heavy linen, twill or
rep in colour and design to
complement needlepoint

30cm (12in) zip (optional)

Thread

38cm (15in) cushion pad

PREPARATION

1 ◆ Mark out an area roughly 39cm
(15½in) × 39cm (15½in) cen-
trally on your canvas using a
permanent marker.
2 ◆ Enlarge the chart by 188% and
place under canvas, to mark out
each area before starting.
3 ◆ Using the chart, start working
the blocks (labelled A to N), working inwards from the outer edge.

▨	900 American Beauty
▨	940 Cranberry
▨	904 American Beauty
▨	312 Grape
▨	311 Grape
▨	D522 Ocean Green
▨	510 Old Blue
☐	342 Periwinkle
▨	341 Periwinkle
▨	553 Ice Blue
☐	522 Teal Blue
▨	D501 Seafarer
▨	500 Federal Blue
☐	503 Federal Blue
▨	571 Navy Blue
▨	952 Strawberry

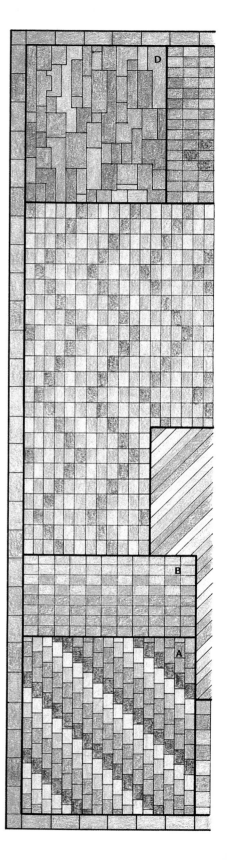

Fill in one block, then go on to the next, working your way around the cushion.

WORKING THE STITCHES

Area A: Worked in a zigzag comprising stepped blocks of 2-thread lengths going in a horizontal direction. Colour order: 940, 311, D501, 342, 510.

Area B: Worked in vertical blocks over 2 threads. Work 4 rows of blocks in alternating 311 and 341, the next 2 rows in 341 and 503, and the last 2 rows in 503 and D501.

Area C: Worked in horizontal blocks of zigzags over 2 threads, each block 3 stitches long. Colour order vertically: 342, 940, D501, 510, 900.

Area D: Worked in random lengths of stitches. Refer to the chart for further detail.

Area E: Worked in vertical blocks over 2 threads, each one 3 stitches wide. Refer to the chart for further detail.

Area F: Worked in vertical zigzag over 2 threads, each block 3 stitches wide. Colour sequence from top left: 940, 312, 510, 341, 500, 940, 900, 311, 500, 341, 940, 510, 900, 341.

Area G: Worked in vertical stripes. Colour order from top left: 900, 510, 312, 940, 500, 311, D501, 500, 341. Repeat this to the corner area.

Area H: Refer to the chart and follow the pattern as shown. The side panels of sloping straight stitch alternate from top in 940 and 571.

Area I: Worked in wide stripes of diagonal colour. Colour order from top left: 510, 341, 500, 940, D501, 571, 900. Repeat to corner area I.

Area J: Worked in horizontal zigzag. Colour order from top of area J: 311, 312, 952, 940, 500. Repeat to the end of this area.

Area K: Refer to the chart and follow the pattern as shown.

Area L: Worked in diagonal stripes in alternating thicknesses of 3-stitch width, then 2-stitch width. Colour order: 311, 522, 342, 952, 940. Continue with this to fill the whole of this panel.

Area M: Worked in large zigzags, using colour 500, with alternating squares in 952, 941, D501, 311 and 940.

Area N: This is a lattice worked in 4 colours. The top stripes are worked in 940, the bottom in 900, the shadow in 571 and the filler in 500.

Border: Work this as shown on the chart.

FINISHING

Block and stretch the finished needlepoint.

MAKING UP

1 ◆ Using the finished needlepoint as a guide, cut the backing fabric, adding a 1.2cm (½in) seam allowance. If a zip is required, then cut the piece as two halves, adding an additional 1.5cm (⅝in) seam allowance on each half for the zip.

2 ◆ If you are using a zip, join the 2 pieces of backing fabric, taking a 1.5cm (⅝in) seam. Stitch the top and bottom 4.5cm (1¾in) of the seam, basting the remaining

30cm (12in). Insert the zip in the basted portion, following the instructions on the packet.

3 ◆ Pin backing to needlepoint

with right sides together. Machine stitch close to needlepoint along 3 of the edges (or all 4 if you have used a zip).

4 ◆ Trim the seam allowance and cut diagonally across the corners, but be careful not to cut too close to the stitching.

5 ◆ Turn the cushion cover right side out. Insert the cushion pad. Close the zip or oversew the open edge by hand.

EXTENDING YOUR RANGE

Broaden your needlepoint 'vocabulary' with these stitches.

TRIPLE CROSS STITCH WITH TENT STITCH

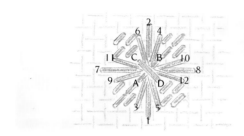

♦ Work the six long stitches on the bottom. Now work a basic cross stitch (see page 23) on top as shown (A-D), using a second colour if desired. Work another triple cross stitch next to this, and fill in the space between with basketweave tent stitch.

WICKERWORK STITCH

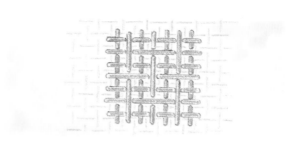

♦ Work **upright cross stitches** over two threads, working back and forth from side to side. Now, in a second colour, make long vertical stitches between them over four threads, and then long horizontal stitches, also over four threads.

LARGE AND STRAIGHT CROSS STITCH

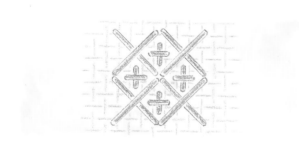

♦ Work four large cross stitches, with each diagonal covering four intersections. Now (in a second colour if desired) in square spaces formed between them, work four **upright cross stitches**, each covering two threads and finishing with the horizontal stitch.

MOORISH STITCH VARIATION

♦ Work a diagonal row of diagonal stitches over one, two then one intersection. For a second diagonal row, using a second needle and a second colour, work **sloping Gobelin stitches** (ie, straight stitches worked diagonally) as shown. Continue alternating rows.

SATIN FLOWER COMBINATION

♦ Make nine **double cross stitches**: for each, work the vertical then the horizontal stitch over four threads, then the two diagonal stitches over two intersections. Fill in with **satin stitch** (satin stitches are stitches worked next to and parallel to each other) in a second colour, over two, three, two, three and then two intersections. In centre, work a Smyrna stitch (see page 55) in a third colour.

FAN STITCH WITH DOUBLE CROSS STITCH

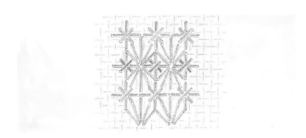

♦ Work nine double cross stitches as for satin flower combination (see left). In spaces between, work fan stitches. To work a fan stitch, make five stitches all sharing one hole. For a neat finish on each, work outer pair of stitches, then inner pair, and finally vertical. The five stitches for the mirror-image fan stitch of the pair (in next row) also share this hole.

LEAF STITCH

♦ This versatile stitch can be used alone or in groups, in pictorial or patterned designs or as a textural background. Work vertical stitch at top first, bringing needle out first at base of it, then work sloping stitches on one side. Now, starting again at top, work other side. New rows interlock so their top stitches butt up to lower stitches of previous row. Sometimes a row of **backstitches** is worked down the centre as a stem: insert needle one horizontal thread behind where it was brought out; bring it out two horizontal threads further on. Continue in same way.

FRENCH KNOTS

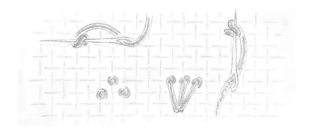

♦ These useful raised stitches can be added to other stitches, used individually, bunched tightly or used over a whole area. Bring needle out one hole below where you want stitch to be, pulling all thread through. Holding thread taut with left hand, wrap thread around needle once and insert needle back in the canvas one thread above original and just to right. To make a French knot on a stalk, follow same procedure but insert needle three or four threads away so the knot forms on top of the stitch.

How Does
Your Garden Grow?

*This final project, a garden sampler, gives you the chance to work
a wide variety of stitches on one piece.*

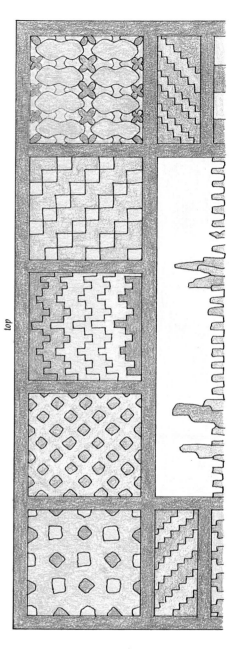

top

SIZE

The unframed picture measures 23cm (9in) × 30.5cm (12in).

STITCHES USED

Satin flower comb. (page 67), Large and straight cross (page 66), Florentine (pages 48-9), Moorish variation (page 66), Fan with double cross (page 67), Straight Gobelin (page 18), Chequer (page 32), Upright cross (page 66), Hungarian (page 38), Triple cross with tent (page 66), Wickerwork (page 66), Brick (page 61), Leaf (page 67), Double cross (page 67), Web (page 37), French knots (page 67), Satin (page 67)

YOU WILL NEED

33cm (13in) × 40.5cm (16in) piece of 10 gauge double-thread canvas

One skein each of Paterna Persian wool listed with the chart (used as 2 threads)

PREPARATION

Enlarge the chart by 140% to the finished size using a photocopier and then place it under your canvas to transfer the outlines. Using the outlines and the chart you will be able to copy the design.

WORKING THE STITCHES

1 ◆ Stitch in cross stitch, over 2 threads, a single row all the way around the outside edge, making sure you have 46 cross stitches at the top and bottom, and 59 on each side.

2 ◆ You will see from the chart that at every following tenth cross stitch on the bottom and the top, the work is sectioned by stitching ten cross stitches (including the stitch in the bottom and top rows), in towards the centre. On the sides the next-to-the-last section going up is divided at the fifth stitch in order to leave the correct space for the top flower bed.

3 ◆ Stitch the inner frame in cross stitch.

4 ◆ Referring to the diagram on page 70 and the chart shown opposite, work each of the flower

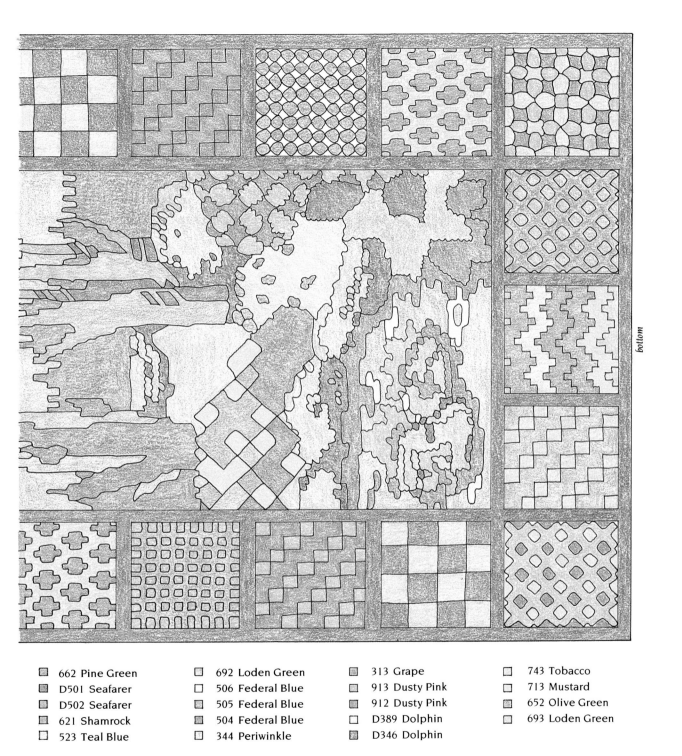

662 Pine Green	692 Loden Green	313 Grape	743 Tobacco
D501 Seafarer	506 Federal Blue	913 Dusty Pink	713 Mustard
D502 Seafarer	505 Federal Blue	912 Dusty Pink	652 Olive Green
621 Shamrock	504 Federal Blue	D389 Dolphin	693 Loden Green
523 Teal Blue	344 Periwinkle	D346 Dolphin	

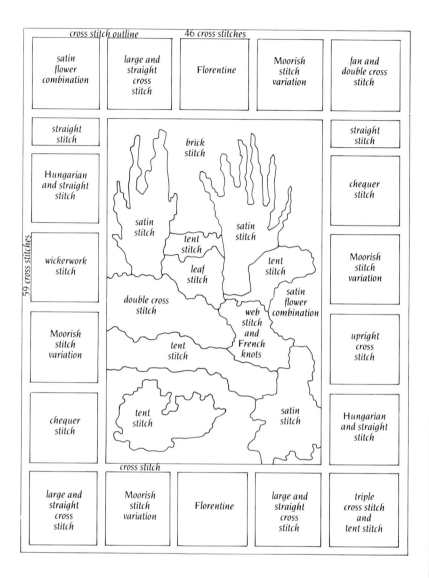

Diagram labels:

cross stitch outline 46 cross stitches

satin flower combination	large and straight cross stitch	Florentine	Moorish stitch variation	fan and double cross stitch

straight stitch

straight stitch

Hungarian and straight stitch

chequer stitch

59 cross stitches

brick stitch

satin stitch

satin stitch

tent stitch

wickerwork stitch

tent stitch

leaf stitch

Moorish stitch variation

double cross stitch

satin flower combination

Moorish stitch variation

web stitch and French knots

upright cross stitch

chequer stitch

tent stitch

tent stitch

satin stitch

Hungarian and straight stitch

cross stitch

large and straight cross stitch	Moorish stitch variation	Florentine	large and straight cross stitch	triple cross stitch and tent stitch

beds surrounding the central garden area.

5 ◆ Again referring to the diagram and the chart, stitch in the central area. If necessary, place your canvas over the chart (if you have enlarged it to the actual size) and, using a permanent marker, roughly mark in the outlines of the different areas in the garden.

FINISHING

Block and stretch the finished needlepoint.

MAKING UP

Either frame the picture or back it with fabric, as directed for the poppies picture on page 44, choosing a fabric that complements the colours in the sampler.

The following stitch symbols are used in the charts in this book.

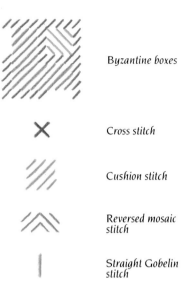

Byzantine boxes

Cross stitch

Cushion stitch

Reversed mosaic stitch

Straight Gobelin stitch

Tent stitch

INDEX

ACKNOWLEDGEMENTS

The author would like to thank the following suppliers for their assistance.

Framecraft Miniatures Ltd, 372–376 Summer Lane, Hockley, Birmingham B19 3QA, for the trinket box and teapot stand. Framecraft have a wide range of products that can be used for needlepoint. Mail order service available; send an SAE for colour brochure.

Paterna, PO Box 1, Ossett, West Yorkshire WF5 9SA, for all the yarns used in the projects. Paterna have an excellent range of over 400 shades of Persian yarns. Telephone (0924) 811905 for details of stockists.